*T*o . . . .

*F*rom . . . .

"If there is anything in my life that can be of value to you, I want you to have it; if I can save you a stumble or a single false step, I want to do it...."

FLORENCE WENDEROTH SAUNDERS

"*Fame is rot; daughters are the thing.*"

J.M. BARRIE (1860-1937),
from "Dear Brutus"

"*I have never had any person in my life
I love as much as my daughter. And I
would trade nothing for her.*"

FRED DEAN

"*Having a daughter is waiting always to see what on earth she's going to do next. How do people without daughters manage? It must be so dull.*"

PAM BROWN, b.1928

"*Daughters do wonderful things.*
Not the wonderful things you expected
them to do.
Different things.
Astonishing things.
Better than you ever dreamed."

MARION C. GARRETTY, b.1917

"*D*ear Daughter. You cost me a fortune in nappies and gripe water; shoes and skirts and hockey sticks. You broke my sleep, you broke my golfing trophy and you nearly broke my heart on several occasions. You were obstinate, noisy, rude, untidy, argumentative, disobedient, lazy - and you backed the car over my geraniums. You read the wrong books, studied the wrong subjects, got the wrong qualifications.
Your boyfriends have been near certifiable.
But you're wonderful.
And I love you. Dad."

DR. PETER SPEARS

"*During the first weeks, I used to lie long hours with the baby in my arms, watching her asleep; sometimes catching a gaze from her eyes: feeling very near the edge, the mystery, perhaps the knowledge of life.*"

ISADORA DUNCAN (1878-1927)

"*In the evening, after she has gone to sleep, I kneel beside the crib and touch her face, where it is pressed against the slats, with mine.*"

JOAN DIDION

"*Suddenly she was here. And I was no longer pregnant; I was a mother. I never believed in miracles before.*"

ELLEN GREENE

"*To show a child what has once delighted you, to find the child's delight added to your own, so that there is now a double delight seen in the glow of trust and affection. This is happiness.*"

J.B. PRIESTLEY (1894-1984)

"*Thank you for giving me back young eyes and a young heart. Thank you for reminding me of summer nights, romance and the taste of peanut butter.*"

PAM BROWN, b.1928

"*The most sophisticated, capable, successful daughter howls for her parents in a crisis. The most modern and socially involved mother or father will drop everything to rush to a daughter in trouble.*"

JANET M. BRIDGES

"My Dear Daughter: Be very good. Do not bump yourself. Do not eat matches. Do not play with scissors or cats. Do not forget your dad. Sleep when your mother wishes it. Love us both. Try to know how we love you. <u>That</u> you will never learn. Good-night and God keep you, and bless you. Your Dad."

RICHARD HARDING-DAVIS

Bright clasp of her whole hand around
my finger,
My daughter, as we walk together now.
All my life I'll feel a ring invisibly
Circle this bone with shining:
when she is grown
Far from today as her eyes are
far already.

STEPHEN SPENDER, b.1909

I would take upon me all for you

Pain me your pain

Your sadness bear

Your tears weep

Mistakes make mine

And shames keep

Deep in my old soul.

Oh that I could for you!

ARNOLD WESKER, b.1932
from "Three Poems for My Daughter Tanya Jo"

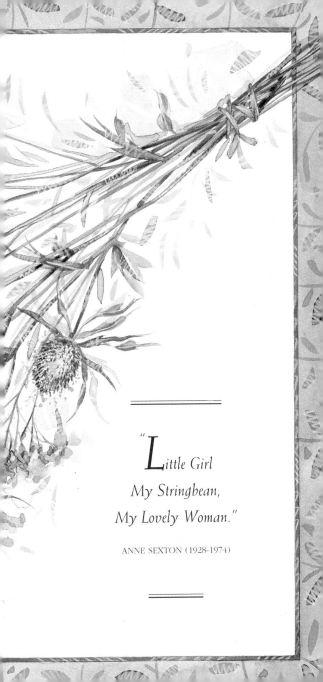

"*Little Girl
My Stringbean,
My Lovely Woman.*"

ANNE SEXTON (1928-1974)

"You are an exceptional person, and a person complete in your own right and must not seek reassurance of a kind which is not of your own fastidious standards. You have no cause to doubt the love Mother and I have for you. In any case it is a belief in your indomitable and singular talent which you must never compromise for others' approval, but follow your own star."

KENNETH ALLSOP, d.1973,
in a letter to his daughter, October 9, 1969

"*Having been fashioned from me
all you do - despite your freedom -
must affect me too.
And so when we're apart
I will always long for news from you.*"

MAYA PATEL, b.1943

"*How lonely the house seems — I never
knew before how well you helped to fill it.*"

FLORENCE WENDEROTH SAUNDERS

*"I hope you find joy in the great things
of life - but also in the little things.
A flower, a song, a butterfly
on your hand."*

ELEN LEVINE

*"Love, peace and an enquiring mind.
That's what I wish for you, my love.
Together with the ability to stand in other
people's shoes. And to laugh at yourself."*

JONATHON A. HUGHES

"*I* wish you all good things - especially the gift of being able to let go. Learn from sorrow and mistakes.

Then go on.

And most of all I wish you courage. That usually takes care of everything else."

PAM BROWN, b.1928

Whatever happens
- fire or flood or cold,
travel or trouble, or just growing old -
our lives are stitched together
by a thread of gold
that cannot change, whatever changes come.
You are my lass forever.

PAM BROWN, b.1928